My Love - Unto Thee!

DR. C.V. Ravindranath

HMCT, PDSHM, MA, MPhil, PhD (Mgmt), PhD (Philo), D. Litt (SQ)

INDIA • SINGAPORE • MALAYSIA

Copyright © DR. C.V. Ravindranath 2025
All Rights Reserved.

ISBN
Paperback 979-8-89744-854-8
Hardcase 979-8-89929-323-8

This book has been published with all efforts taken to make the material error-free after the consent of the author. However the author and the publisher do not assume and hereby disclaim any liability to any party for any loss damage or disruption caused by errors or omissions whether such errors or omissions result from negligence accident or any other cause.

While every effort has been made to avoid any mistake or omission, this publication is being sold on the condition and understanding that neither the author nor the publishers or printers would be liable in any manner to any person by reason of any mistake or omission in this publication or for any action taken or omitted to be taken or advice rendered or accepted on the basis of this work. For any defect in printing or binding the publishers will be liable only to replace the defective copy by another copy of this work then available.

Our Sincere thanks

ॐ Maha Tripura Sundariye Namah:

Sri Adi Shankaracharya

Curriculum Vitae of DR. C.V.Ravindranath,
HMCT, PDSHM, MA, MPhil, PhD (Mgmt), PhD (Philo), D. Litt (SQ).

Vision and Mission Statement of DR. C.V. Ravindranath

Vision: Purity * Creativity * Spirituality

Mission: Wisdom * Wellness * Wealth

            (Saraswati)   (Parvati)   (Laxmi)

I Birth:

C.V. Ravindranath was born in Colombo to an affluent family of Jewellers, ISLAND GOLD HOUSE, which was recognized by Her Majesty Queen Elizabeth of England. He is a virgoan, born on 24th August, 1954 at 9 pm – Punnartham Nakshathram; in Ratna Hospital, Colombo, Ceylon.

II Alumni:

1. St. Teresa's Anglo-Indian Convent – Kindergarten (Baby class) – 1960.

2. St. Michael's Anglo-Indian Boys' High School, Kannur- Anglo-Indian Schools Examination, Chennai (1961-1971) Madras Board of Anglo-Indian Examinations.

3. P.S.G College of Technology, Coimbatore – Pre-Technical (1972-1973).

4. Birla Institute of Technology and Science (BITS) Pilani, Rajasthan – 1st B Tech (Hons) - (1973-1974) (Discontinued due to extreme cold climate).

5. Institute of Hotel Management, Catering Technology and Applied Nutrition, Mumbai- HMCT, PDSHM (1976-1980).

6. Cornell University, School of Hotel Administration, USA – Hotel Sales & Marketing (1983).

7. Gemological Institute of America (GIA), USA – Fine Jewellery Sales Consultant (1991).

8. Indian Diamond Institute (IDI), Surat – Diamond – Sales (1992).

9. Indian Institute of Management (IIM), Ahmedabad – SMEP (2000).

10. Indian Institute of Kozhikode, MDP (2001).

11. Regional Engineering College & Management studies – MDP (2002).

12. Madurai Kamaraj University, Madurai – MA & MPhil (2004-2006).

13. Indian School of Business – (ISB) Hyderabad – MDP (2007).

14. Kannur University, Dept. of Philosophy, PhD – The Prospects of Meditative Techniques in Transforming Socio–Personal Domains of Fundamentalism (2008-2013).

15. International Open University, Colombo, Honorary PhD in SQ in Business Management (2014).

16. Academy for Spiritual Scientist – Kingship Academy: Honorary Doctorate in Spirituality (2015).

Preface

My Love Unto Thee, the beautiful collection of 18 poems, expresses in each one, the poet's passion and versatility. The poems, each one exclusive in its feature, varied in nature, cover spirituality to patriotism, love to realization.  This gallery of amazing literature is just like a garden overflowing with colourful flowers, where in "The Peace Within' forms a bouquet of roses. For the multi-talented and dynamic personality that Ravi ji is, poetry seems to be THE PATH that takes him closest to GOD / Self-realization.

Manisha, B.Com, M.Com

Foreword

The Collection of Poems named, "My Love - Unto Thee" by Dr. C.V. Ravindranath portrays the love that is pure, divine and eternal, unconfined by societal differences. It celebrates the Universality of love - A love free from bondage and not constrained by religious  doctrines and dogmas, allowing for a blissful union that leads to true realisation and enlightenment. This kind of love recognizes all beings as children of the same superconscious power. The poet delves deeply into the essence of spirituality, conveying the message that true inner peace comes from within oneself, rather than through external worldly pleasures.

The poems "Feelings of Love" and "Flight of Love" envision love as a transformative force. The relation between light dispelling darkness and love overcoming hatred is inspiring. The poet depicts the healing power of love that can wipe away the tears of misery and transform a basic instinct into a spiritual awakening. "Ocean of Love – Unto Thee" emphasises the ocean's characteristics of glory, vastness, timelessness and tranquility mirroring the qualities and nature of love. The poems "India My Love" and "God's Own Country" reflect the rich cultural and spiritual heritage of our Motherland, capturing its essence by blending history and contemporary issues into a powerful narrative of love and hope. The poet celebrates the beauty of a woman in poems like "Country Girl", 'Tempest' and 'Picnic' in unique ways, reflecting on various dimensions of beauty through joy, simplicity, innocence and wilderness, relating them to nature. Similarly "Love Affair" is a mesmerising journey through the mystical and passionate connection between nature and love.

"Tears of Love" delves into the profound impact of religious and ideological conflicts of humanity, the rise of militancy, terrorism, fanaticism and fundamentalism, which have led to the suffering of innocent children. Similarly in the poem "War and Love" he criticises the brutality of war conveying a strong condemnation of the leaders who instigate conflict for their gain, disregarding the lives they destroy. It reinforces the message that only love and compassion are the ultimate paths to harmony and unity. Themes of unity and equality are also prevalent throughout the poem "The New Man", with a strong emphasis on overcoming divisions based on religion, caste, creed and colour.

"Peace within" beautifully captures the journey of finding peace within oneself rather than seeking it through external forces. Similarly "Glimpse of blue sky" symbolises clarity and peace, inspiring a journey toward inner serenity and purpose."

"Secret of Secrets" presents the idea that true love and bliss come from transcending the dualities of the mind and from worldly desires and conflict and connecting with a deeper, existential truth. "Tears! Roll back..." reminds us that true happiness comes from counting our blessings appreciating what we have and finding joy in love and friendship. In "Flight of Ecstasy" the poet takes readers on a captivating journey through the chakras, exploring the spiritual and energetic centres of the human body, from the base of the spine to the pinnacle of enlightenment. In "Love Play" the poet suggests that physical pleasure is just momentary, while deep meditation allows for a profound merging of these energies, leading to a state of ultimate bliss.

Each poem reflects the poet's vision of purity, creativity, spirituality and divinity serving as a gentle reminder of the beauty and love that exists within and around us.

Dear reader, I hope these poems touch your heart as profoundly as they touched ours.

ॐ Adi Paraashaktiye Namah:

Sanita R, BHM, MBA (USA)

Reviews on

'My Love- Unto Thee'

1. C.V. Ravindranath explores the realm of love in all its magnitudes and paints his lyrical canvas with colours of love a new.

   ➢ **Mark Sykes**
   Editor in Chief,
   Minerva Press, London

2. The sentiments are charming I'm touched to have a dedicated copy.

   ➢ **Sue Bradbury**
   Editorial Director,
   The Folio Society, London.

3. The collection of the poems truly reveals the profound multifaceted understanding of life. In particular, we would like to make mention of the poem 'Tears of Love', which is pertinent in the present context, when the human civilization is entrapped in the turmoil of 'Terrorism and hatred'.

   ➢ **A Faria** General Manager
   D. Chandavarker
   Divisional Manager,
   Daimler Chrysler India Pvt. Ltd.
   (Makers of Mercedes Benz cars in India).

4. Surely, it makes interesting reading. I especially liked 'Peace within'.

> **Capt. C.P. Krishnan Nair**
>
> Chairman
>
> Hotel Leela Venture Ltd. Mumbai.

5. I have gone through the book "My Love- Unto Thee" and it makes a very interesting reading.

> **R.K. Krishnakumar**
>
> Vice-Chairman,
>
> Taj Group of Hotels, Mumbai.

6. Poetry takes you towards God and it is a good form of Sadhana

> **Swamini Vimalananda**
>
> President
>
> Chinmaya International School,
> Coimbatore.

7. "My Love- Unto Thee", Keeps up lofty thoughts.

> **Swami Chidananda**
>
> President
>
> Chinmaya International Foundation.

8. The Poems written by Ravindranath are excellent

> **Dr. P.C. Thomas**
>
> Good Sheppard International School
> Ooty.

9. The poems are really beautiful, good work!

   ➢ **Dr. P. Rajendran M.S.**

   F.R.C.S (EDIN) FRCS (GLAS),

   Calicut.

10. They are beautifully composed with human touch and feelings. Each one is so different from the other.

    ➢ **K. Ramadasan**

    National Institute of Oceanography

    Dona Paula.

11. A Poet whose creativity is still at the tip of his fingers could only write such hearty poems.

    ➢ **Dr. M.O. Mini,** Kannur

12. It was indeed a unique achievement by an Indo-Anglian poet comparable only to the establishment of a world record by a debutant athlete.

    ➢ **Mr. N.K. Krishnan Master.**

13. Dr. C.V. Ravindranath has been working tirelessly for the betterment of society.

    This compilation of poems aims to engender love and compassion and embodies the spirit of the author.

    ➢ **Mr. Sean Clarke,** Maharshi Adhyatma Vishwavidyalay, Goa, India.

14. Dr. Ravindranath ji is revealing the Power of The All Pervading One through his poems. His works motivate the readers to cast away negative tendencies and lead a meaningful life. He inspires people to dedicate their lives in the protection and preservation of our culture and tradition. I appreciate Dr. Ravindranath Ji for bringing forth such thought provoking poems.

   ➤ **Swamini Devi Jnanabha Nishta,** Santhananda Mutt Rishi Jnana Sadhanalayam, Sree Santhananda Vidya Nikethan, Pathanamthitta, Kerala

Contents

Feelings of Love

Darkness can never be fought-
How can we fight with darkness?
Only light can remove it!

So too with hatred,
It can be removed by love,
Only by love alone!

Love is not a relationship,
But a state of mind of friendship.

Love always flows from the hearts,
Never from the head where ego rests.

Heart is the only weapon,
Mankind knows to transform the demon.

Like light enkindles another,
Millions of hearts together,
Enlighten our culture!

If love is the only language of the heart
Through which God speaks,
Then let us speak forever by Heart!

8th Dec 1999

Flight of Love

Love flies on the wings of freedom,
To live a life without boredom.

Love lives in the deepest ocean of heart,
Where it flows outward not to hurt.

But only to soothe and wipe,
The tears of misery and hope.

Love transforms the basic instinct,
Where the serpent sleeps in lust.

To awaken the inner energy to joy,
Where mankind can find its glory.

Where it sparkles on the spiritual peak,
A lotus of thousand petals blooms to seek.

The pleasure of terrestrial joy,
Take off on the golden flight of fantasy.

Where the soul disappears into cosmic,
To the tunes of His Heavenly music.

9th Dec 1999

Ocean of Love – Unto Thee!

Deep down in the valley,
Burst the highest peak of ecstasy!

Where the mind stills to nobody,
When the heart pours all glory.

Love overwhelms the timeless space,
To the highest joy of human race.

There we dance with nature,
To the beats of the Almighty power.

Flowers bloom to shower,
Downpour the nectar.

The fountain of joy sparkles in power,
Each drop trickles down to the river.

Drinking the snowy dews of nature,
The raving ocean roars in the merger.

When the golden red sun kisses,
The trembling lips of the waves.

We are washed away on the shore,
Where our footprints lay no more!

10th Dec 1999

India My Love

India my love lies in glory,
Resting her head high, majestically,
The great Himalayas of tranquility!

The waves of her wisdom flow verily,
Like the curly locks of the divine pageantry,
Ganga, Yamuna and Saraswati!

Her face so charming and lovely,
Like the blossoming flowers of Kashmiri,
As fresh as the green paddy of Punjabi!

Her golden heart traces the reigns of dynasty,
The crowned nerve centre, the rule of Delhi,
Where Taj, Qutab and Red Fort resound historically!

From her womb sprouts the seed of ecstasy,
The thoughts of Vedas and Upanishads spiritually,
Krishna, Rama, Buddha and Mahavira proclaimed
worldly!

Suckled the wisdom of her bosom, the great saints
meditatively,
Patanjali, Sankara and Vivekananda spoke
universally,
To make the world one, a big family!

At her navel, the stones of Khajuraho dancingly,
Teach the crowd the lower instinct naturally,
To be risen to the highest peak of joy eternally!

On her right beholds the Karma Yogi,
The wealthy children of Gujarat and Mumbai,
Like Tata, Birla, Bajaj and Ambani!

On her left folds the fist of revolutionary,
Where their thoughts are painted in red and fury,
Yet Tagore overshines in Art and Poetry!

Deep down in the ocean are the feet of Kanyakumari,
Dancing and singing the classics of Carnatic and
Madrasi,
Where her holy lotus feet are washed tributarily!

Her teachings are simple, yet grave,
To behold, we should be more brave,
Love and only love pure shall survive!

All are perishable but only the soul,
Unto thee, we meditate be the goal,
Let thy kingdom come, be eternal!

Never did she give birth to the bad and mad,
Like Genghis, Hitler, Stalin and Mao had,
Taken the world in bloodshed and tortured!

Never did she conquer another's earth,
Nor she plundered another's wealth,
Non-violence had become her mental sheath!

Many a wicked captured her might,
Only to loot and steal her wealth,
Moghuls, French and English head the list!

For all those who are at crest and cross,
She shared all her prize and wise,
To make them all great and rise!

Never did she convert for race and rice,
Making her culture bright thrice,
Enlightening and inspiring her spiritual voice!

Indeed, such a beauty my country, Motherly,
India my love, dancing and singing divinely,
Awaken the universal brotherhood spiritually!

8th Jan 2000

Country Girl

Country girl charming and rare,
Dancing and singing unaware.

Her words are soft, foolish too,
Sparkling eyes innocent two.

Strawberry cheeks of moonlight night,
Trembling lips of sunset bright.

Fluttering breeze her curly hair,
Blossoming buds a lovely pair.

Raving curves of swinging wear,
Gushing blood of raging fair.

Screaming with joy, her moment's trace,
Spurts of ecstasy shower the Divine's grace.

She has no past to bury, future to hurry,
Living in His presence, never to worry.

Her mind is blank, but heart is full,
God's great gift of love, so beautiful!

4th Jan 2000

Tears of Love!

Krishna was never a Hindu Brahmin,
Christ was never a Roman Christian,
But Priests and saints converted their identity,
Confusing the evil minds to fight fundamentally!

Militancy and terrorism became their Quran to corrupt,
Superstition and fundamentalism became their Bible
to fright,
Fanaticism and communalism have made Gita out of
sight,
Mankind has lost the love for their hearts to fight!

Unto this chaos our children suffocate,
Horrifying attacks on their kith and kin separate,
Time may cleanse the stains of their bloodshed,
But the scars of tears on their cheeks never hide!

The wound is so deep where vengeance is sowed,
Let the whole world unite to combat this evil to end,
The need of the time is the essence of the spirit,
Let us break their mad laws by striking them hard!

Love and only universal love can unite our souls,
Which mankind has lost its heart in doctrines,
Let meditation be the new millennium's prize,
Only to enkindle that eternal light to bliss!

The Church shall stop its slavery beliefs,
The Mosque shall strip its barbarian rules,
Provocation at Mandir shall be at ease,
Holy or unholy Jihad will be forced to cease!

May the Heaven shower the flowers of blessings,
For the marathon task to save earthly beings,
Let the great powers of the globe bestow love and
peace,
Making our beloved earth, a better place for living
beings!

23rd Jan 2000

The New Man!

Throwing away the lunatic scriptures of the mad,
The new man shall turn to nature to guard.
Never to be chained by any church, mosque or temple,
Nor to hear any preach of the priest to slave!

Never to chip off his skin anymore to grade,
Nor to submerge in the water to change,
Breaking the cross belt of upholding the pride,
He shall turn all logs of dogmas into fire to rise!

Rising above the mind it shall burn bright to light.
The glory of the new millennium, the wisdom might!
Mankind then shall find his birthright,
To live in this world henceforth, without any fright!

Religion then shall not be his ultimate limit,
Line of control shall not be his dying pit,
Caste, creed and colour will be made to rest,
Compassion and love shall be at the best!

Onto the wings of love and freedom,
Mankind shall fly unto wisdom,
The godliness of man shall rise to shower,
The fragrance of peace and tranquil shall flower!

The man-made Gods in the cage shall die to doom,
The godliness of the souls shall live to bloom,
Fundamentalism shall ruin to a withered broom,
Spiritualism shall win all souls to groom!

Then he shall behold all as the manifestation of
Nature,
The children of the same superconscious power,
Birds, trees and stones shall sing of this lover,
Eternally sleep, O man, in their spiritual prayer.

22nd Jan 2000

Glimpse of the Blue Sky!

When life gets tough,
And your journey becomes rough,

An Eagle's look and Lion's will,
Shall remove all your silly ill,

Get detached like a pumpkin,
From the winding creeper on the pine.

When the faults are many,
Yet sins you do not have any,

Keep your head high,
Never lose your smile with sigh,

Have a glimpse of the blue sky,
Without black clouds any.

Never be bothered about your future,
Never be worried about your past err,

Live each moment of today,
Like a rainbow of the day,

Spreading love and glory
Of the master of this canopy.

Alone, I sit on the shore with a weary eye,
Watching your feats to glorify,

And with all hopes not lost I cry to thee;
Help this child my Lord to be a glory to me!

Make her life so sublime,
Leaving footprints on the sands of time,

On the shore where I sit and smile,
Awaiting my tears to hide,

To have a glimpse of the sky,
Without any clouds on it to shy!

28th June 2000

Peace Within

Life never clicks out of the clock,
Tomorrow never flicks out of the walk,
Where the two hands march like a soldier,
As the custodian's of your life's saviour!

Hope is greater than reality,
When misery strikes life slightly,
Importance of tomorrow overrides today suddenly,
To postpone your moments of life abruptly!

Sum total of your yesterdays and today,
Will be the tomorrow your longing day,
Which your hope welcomes day by day,
Until you blame the Gods for your birthday!

Life is not a joke to blame others,
It is a game to be played otherwise,
Whether be misery or happiness, it is all yours,
Enjoy it thoroughly as the spring of the summer rains!

Ego the root cause of all evils and miseries,
Which hides in vain all your peace,
Stop your search for peace outside else,
And delve inside you to get its grace!

By marching a soldier you shall not win over the
bridge,
Nor by plundering others you shall gain any edge,
Never can mankind be in peace,
By waging a bloody war in disgrace!

Deep beneath you it sleeps within you,
Beyond the rustle and bustle mind in you,
Where you can glimpse the sparkle in you,
Like a rainbow on a sunny dew!

Peace profound is within you, your inner self,
Your true nature is the goal itself,
Knifing a heart shall not glorify thyself,
Peace is in your hands and serve above self!

29th June 2000

Tears! Roll back...

School fete a great joy of pride,
Lots of fun and frolic to take a ride,
Charming girls and prizes galore,
For those who have spare money to explore!

I looked out of the window to catch their store,
Because I do not have any pie to spare,
Not even a pair of shoes to wear,
I wept like a baby which mothers' bear!

Drops of tears trickling down the cheeks cannot hold,
Because they bear the anguish of the poverty bold,
Down to earth I cursed my breed,
Up above the sky I cried for the creed!

I wept and wept for a pair of shoes,
Until I saw a man without any legs,
Holding to the window grills,
Pleaded God for never such chills!

Jumped out of the house by praying,
Ran to the school, saw my little brother playing,
Without a single pie, never bothering,
Sharing an ice cream, running and screaming!

Friends came running, vying each other,
To take me in their fold for a get-together,
Unto their love I forgot my sorrows to bother,
Rolling back my tears, never to be a pauper!

30th June 2000

The Tempest

Up in the galleria to behold the colours,
The storm of the brush which washes the throbbing
hearts,
Where the painter dissolves into the paints,
Like a dancer disappearing into her steps!

Colours and colours of rainbow bright,
Unto that fantasy of the divine great,
Where everyone gets enlightened to His light,
Except Man for his petty fight!

Onto the canvas of nature's blue,
I caught hold of a damsel in her natural hue,
Decked in leaves which nature grew,
Crowned with flowers of summer dew!

Her starry eyes twinkled like a full moon blue,
Her rosy lips smack like ripples flow,
Her blooming blossoms where honey bees flew,
When a gush of wind rip her beauty true!

Stunned by the beauty of nature's art,
Caught in the whirlwind of the craving heart,
Where man shall leap to the highest height,
Of fantasy and ecstasy clinging to their peakiest tight!

Pondering and pondering to behold that face,
Which time had tickled off out of trace,
From the memory of the lover's grace,
Now only agony remains in life's race!

Hours together I remained in her praise,
Forgetting myself in the crowd so peace,
Until I heard a voice at such a raise,
Saw my wife losing her patience all in a craze!

A gush of storm passes across like a flight,
A fleet of love birds flew in a plight,
Saddened with anguish she yelled outright,
"Are you waiting for winter to set or what?"

20th July 2000

God's Own Country!

As a slim damsel attired in green,
Lush coconut palms waved in serene,
Greeting her lover to her terrain,
On the golden beaches of her shrine!

She was created by a myth of golden axe,
By the great sage of golden age,
Parasurama in his moments of rage,
God's own country thus came to age!

Like a womb the tiny blue lagoon lie,
Where the great saints of wisdom high,
Sankara, Narayana, Chattambi,
Chinmaya, Nithyananda and Amrithanandamayi,
Came to world to teach the Spiritual joy!

Such learned was my land of hills,
Until the wicked mind of red thoughts,
Corrupted our children with blood stains,
Bleeding our hearts on our cultural ruins!

To save the courtyard which holy threads hold,
The cross-eyed boy spoke in trembling bold,
Taking the sweating class for a ride,
As a landlord to rule them still deprived!

Unto these miseries every Keralites live,
Hoping for the good their high literacy slave,
Awaiting these bad guys doom to grave,
To bring back those past glories alive!

By knifing a soul, the poor shall not enrich,
Until the mad politicians' mind shall switch,
From the greed of wealth to spirituality, which,
Make God's own country splendidly rich!

The Devil's own workshop shall come to halt,
Tampering the innocent minds to revolt,
Leading our future, our children shall tilt,
Towards God's own country bright!

Renaissance shall be thy name to light,
Religions shall stop their crazy fight,
Malayalees shall then take a glorious flight,
To their own country, where we shall have our
birthright!

24th Aug 2000

Love Affair

Clandestine gleam overwhelms the ocean,
Candid wind whispers to the swinging maiden,
Smoky black locks wear a platinum crown,
Unto that silvery silence I am madden!

The moonlit beam pulls the waves up and down,
Like a lunatic damsel dancing to her own tune,
Fluttering her attire to meet her beloved in vain,
Lost to the conditioned world of silly gain!

Stars manifested a spectacular burst,
Like the painter's stroke the colours bright,
Lost to the love the beloved outburst,
To those mystic tunes of thunderous beat!

Dark blue canopy shatters into million lights,
Lush green palms could not bear their streaks,
Sensuous waves sprout their lips for smacks,
Unto the ecstasy of everlasting moments!

Onto those ripples I rolled on and on,
On her panting bosom the waves roll on,
Bouncing hither and thither I jumped on,
Lost to the whirlpool of joyous cyclone!

The life force nectar starts drizzling insane,
Like a dewdrop trickling on a summer rain,
Stretching her arms she yelled in vain,
In that timeless space of her inner shrine!

Encircling the nature the cosmic energy drain,
Unto that womb of Mother Nature remain,
When the golden flower blooms to brighten,
Like thousand suns rise to lighten!

A Lotus of thousand petals blossom in joy,
Seeds of existence sprout in glory,
Gazing the full moon still glowing far away,
I still lie on the wet sands to glorify.

5th Nov 2000

Secret of Secrets

Human mind always strives in duality,
Double-sided coin in your complexity,
You utter ugly, it thinks of beauty,
You say sad, it longs to be happy,
Triggering millions of thoughts in weary!

Mind is cunning and powerful too,
It gathers momentum, when it splits into two,
If you hear, it cajoles the listener to woe,
When you look, it curtails the seer as a foe,
The unbridled wild horses of senses in four!

Right mind is feminine, joyously being receptive,
Left mind is masculine, powerfully being creative,
Each one of them passing like a cloud sedative,
Striking three-quarters of your time alternative,
Until you tame them to merge as a whole selective!

When compassion and love in you pervade,
Thy left nostril shall take turn to breathe,
When ego and power crave you to entangle,
Thy right one shall gasp to exhale,
Always opposite to the mind thou shall respire!

Unto its atrocities man is allowed to grow,
Unwanted rubbish it accumulates to brew,
The conditioning of political, religious and social
draw,
The past miseries and future anxieties flow,
Thus mankind has gained no peace, but sorrow!

She and he shall not meet, rather,
Only at split moments together,
When the life energy strikes over,
At the pinnacle where ecstasy shall shower,
Until yin and yang converge into one another!

Silence can alter the pattern of breath,
Thoughts shall reside in tranquil worth,
State of no mind then thou shall earth,
Quantum leap shall be thy new birth,
Where million orgasms shall be your wealth!

The greatest lover is the one to be sure,
Who needs no beloved anymore,
Whose need for love is with existential true,
Beyond mind delving in its own source deeper,
And unto this divine bliss, I embrace thee my dear!

9th Nov 2000

War and Love

Snow-clad mountains drenched in bloody bath,
Like the daggered bosom of motherly earth,
Where her children are sacrificed for no worth,
For the sake of politicians who have blind faith!

War is the holocaust of the sick mind,
Where their inferiority complex screw to wind,
Vested interests are their ultimate vend,
Ulterior motive to snatch stinking fund!

On the tombs of idiots' cemetery,
Name shall be lettered in the history,
When they are massacred in politicians' butchery,
Depriving many a love and joy in thy family!

Beloved has lost her life partner,
Wife got widowed from her husband's care,
Mothers weep at their sons' departure,
Cheeks of innocence are scarred with tears!

Wound so deep where seeds of vengeance sprint,
Mankind should learn to control the mind vagrant,
Collective responsibility drives men to stunt,
When their leader's tongue lashes out to vent!

War is a war full of bloodshed and killing,
Alas nobody winning and no one losing,
Man in his inner core should start thinking,
To serve humanity with love invoking!

Erase all those stupid lines of control,
To make our sweet earth free for all,
Spreading compassion each and for all,
Without any prejudice of religious rule!

Love is a miracle, thy greatest attitude,
Give out Love, thy heartiest plentitude,
Then whole existence shall shower in multitude,
Benediction of thousandfold will be thy beatitude!

The hands which have rocked the cradle of love,
Cannot touch a gun loaded with deadly grave,
Awaken spiritually my brethren so brave,
To remove those tears, for peace to survive!

11th Nov 2000

Flight of Ecstasy

Welcome on board, the Flight of Ecstasy!
Ladies and gentlemen,
Fasten your seatbelts,
For the take-off,
From the base,

MULADHARA CHAKRA – Earth Element!
Close your eyes and meditate........

Tip of the spine end lies Muladhara, the birth chakra,
Serpent of Kundalini, the life energy aura,
Hereditary traits descend from thy birth era,
Coiled force of lust to set free sexuality supra,
Psychosomatic emotions transcend spiritual flora!

Arrival at
SWADHISHTHANA CHAKRA – Water Element!

Swadhisthana, the death chakra lies above Sex Centre,
Etheric body where all emotions enter,
Moving above the basic instincts shall render,
Great human qualities of intellectual wonder,
Alas, millions die at animalistic yonder!

Arrival at
MANIPURA CHAKRA – Fire Element!

At the naval lies Manipura, the astral body,
Diamond chakra sparkles trust to intellectual body,
Expressions of relaxed mind shall be ready,
Dancing and singing of thy aesthetic joyously,
Having glimpse of the blue sky silently!

Arrival at
ANAHATHA CHAKRA – Air Element!

Anahatha Chakra, centre of Tantra physiology,
At the heart where love overwhelms universally,
A determined vision of psychic body,
Where humming of Om vibrates mentally,
When ego melts by warmth of love heartily!

Arrival at
VISHUDDHA CHAKRA – Sky Element!

Love purifies all impurities of this spiritual body,
Vishuddha chakra at the throat signifies purity,
Thou shall have the godly speech of clarity,
Purity of thy soul spreads magnetic serenity,
Bringing peace and solace to the whole humanity!

Arrival at
AGYA/AJNA CHAKRA – Self Consciousness!

When the life energy reaches Ajna between the eyebrows,
Thy third eye shall open to pure consciousness,
Where thy cosmic body shall shower spiritual bliss,
God's Will shall be your Will of true existence,
Thou shall be the master of all universal truths!

Arrival at
SAHASRARA CHAKRA - ॐ Shiva – Shakti ॐ :

Pinnacle point of ultimate, the nirvanic body,
Thousand suns rise to lighten the infinity,
To enlighten thy non-existence of no body,
Above the pineal, different reality shall signify,
A lotus of thousand petals shall bloom to glorify!

Krishna called it 'Sat Chit Ananda'.
Saraha called it 'Pure Love'.
Patanjali called it 'Samadhi'.
Buddha called it 'Nirvana'.
Jesus called it 'Thy kingdom come'.
Modern philosophy terms it 'Pure-Consciousness'.
Science may discover it as 'Cosmic energy'.

Because Shankara Sang Shivoham ! Shivoham !!

Ladies and Gentlemen,
Loosen your seatbelts,
The Flight of Ecstasy,
Has landed...

11th Nov 2000

Love Play

Conscious mind in man is male,
While unconscious a female,
Polar opposite they trail!

Conscious mind in woman is female,
While unconscious a male,
Polar opposite they hail!

When he and she meet bodily,
Orgasm is just momentary,
Only a glimpse of spirituality!

But in deep meditation both merge single,
And deep orgasms of compassion sprinkle,
Showering highest bliss possible!

Meeting of yin and yang in unity,
Merging of love in Shiva and Shakthi,
Greatest of all love play eternally!

You may call it Maha Samadhi,
A state of blissfulness of nothingness,
Alas, sex transcends to spirituality!

Unto it, Sweetheart, Let's meditate...

12th Nov 2000

Picnic

Bus loaded with fun ablaze in screams,
Joyous moments of youthful freak-outs,
Music is only but organised noises,
Life's best times of intimate voices!

Blue lagoon looked afresh and youthful,
As the waves dancing so agile and playful,
Slim palms kept the rhythm so graceful,
Like a teacher, the Sun was very watchful!

Sweating and panting we ran to the palm grove,
Where delicious treat welcome to serve,
Behind the delicacy I behold in crave,
I caught hold of winking eyes inviting love!

A gush of wind blew her golden locks,
For me to glance her glamorous looks,
Deep vibrations exchange waves with no words,
A great longing deep-rooted in our little hearts!

The ocean looked so silent and virgin,
Perplexed when our first love origin,
Lost to the world the sun got driven,
Into the gasping warmth of love's ocean!

Unto those golden waves she ran to the sea,
When the giggling girls flock to see,
To hide her heart's temptations flee,
Like a skylark tracing his fiancée!

A storming wave pulled her across,
Leaving us all on the shore at cross,
Running to her rescue the tides embarrass,
The waves have snatched her to our surprise!

Helpless we stood on the sands so grave,
To witness the goodbye! her hands wave,
Until my tears washed her sight so alive,
My first love in vain sleep, never to die!

The journey of life is with no expectations,
Living here and now with no desires,
Weather abruptly changes the silent waves,
Like the bus loaded with fun returned in sighs!

18th Nov 2000

Mahamerus Designed by Dr. C.V. Ravindranath

Shree Yantra Mahameru	
Shiva – Shakti Mahameru	
Sri Kali Yantra Mahameru	
ॐ Shiva – Shakti ॐ Mahameru	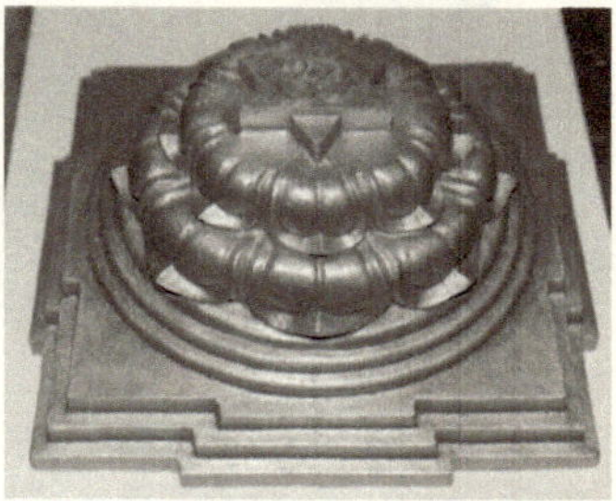

സത്യം • ജ്ഞാനം • ധർമ്മം • കർമ്മം • അർത്ഥം

KISNA

INDIA'S FIRST
BIS CERTIFIED JEWELLER

INDIA'S FIRST BIS CERTIFIED JEWELLER
THE TORCH BEARER OF GOLD PURITY IN INDIA

Krishna Jewels

Thavakkara, Kannur -670001, Kerala, India
+91 497 2767465, 2766515, 2764514, 2764516, 2702467 8281100514
sudhacvr@gmail.com www.krishnajewelsindia.com krishnajewelskannur krishnajewelskannur

DIAMONDS ARE FOR ALL AND FOREVER !

സത്യം • ജ്ഞാനം • ധർമ്മം • കർമ്മം • അർത്ഥം

KISNA

adithi devo bhava

WORLD'S FIRST RESORT BUILT ON
TANTRIC VAASTU SHILPA SHASTHRA

SPIRITUAL - HEALTH WELLNESS TOURISM
adithi devo bhava:
Krishna Beach Resort
REJUVENATION OF BODY MIND SOUL
BY AYURCARE, YOGA, TANTRA & KALARI

Payyambalam, Palliyamoola, Kannur-8, Kerala, India
0497 2715888   7558887704   reservations@kbrkannur.com,
krishnabeachresort.knr@gmail.com, gm@kbrkannur.com, www.kbrkannur.com krishnabeachresort

Rejuvenation of Body - Mind - Soul

സത്യം • ജ്ഞാനം • ധർമ്മം • കർമ്മം • അർത്ഥം

Shivoham Spiritual Wellness Centre
Krishna Beach Resort, Palliyamoola, Kannur Presents:

LIFESTYLE HEALTH PACKAGE
FOR THE REJUVENATION OF BODY, MIND AND SOUL

For Booking: 7558887704   0497 2715888

reservations@kbrkannur.com / krishnabeachresort.knr@gmail.com/agm@kbrkannur.com 7558887704 www.kbrkannur.com

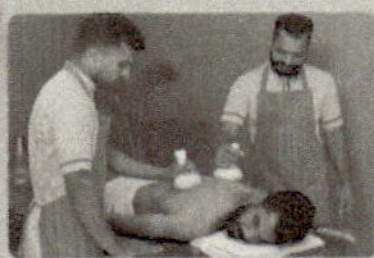
AYURVEDA MASSAGE

KALARIPAYATTU

YOGA

ENHANCE YOUR HAPPY HORMONES SUCH AS DOPAMINE,
SEROTONIN, OXYTOCIN, ENDORPHIN AND MELATONIN THROUGH AYUR CARE,
YOGA, KALARIPAYATTU AND TANTRA.

We Care Spiritual Wellness Tourism

INDIA'S FIRST BIS CERTIFIED JEWELLER
THE TORCH BEARER OF GOLD PURITY IN INDIA
Krishna Jewels
Thavakkara, Kannur -670001, Kerala, India
+91 497 2767465, 2786515, 2764514, 2764516, 2702467 8281100514
sudhacvr@gmail.com www.krishnajewelsindia.com
krishnajewelskannur krishnajewelskannur

SPIRITUAL - HEALTH WELLNESS TOURISM
adithi devo bhava
Krishna Beach Resort
REJUVENATION OF BODY MIND SOUL
BY AYURCARE, YOGA, TANTRA & KALARI
Payyambalam - Palliyamoola Kannur-8 Kerala India
0497 2715888 7558887704
reservations@kbrkannur.com, krishnabeachresort.knr@gmail.com
agm@kbrkannur.com www.kbrkannur.com krishnabeachresort

Buy Jewellery at Krishna Jewels to win a Honeymoon suite at Krishna Beach Resort.

A Spiritual Ecstasy of Tantric Creativity!
Save our Children from Drug Abuses for Good Brain Health and Growth!

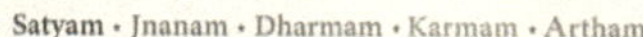

With the blessings of **Jagadguru Sri Adi Shankaracharya**

ॐ Shiva - Shakti Pendant

Available in Gold, Silver & Copper
for positive energy - Peace & Prosperity.

Energy report on the ॐ **Shiva - Shakti Pendant of Maharishi University of Spirituality** Research Team, Goa, dt.11.9.2023

1. **Universal Aura Scan reading:** Positive aura of 9.84 metres in copper.
2. **Subtle analysis:** The pendant emits positive energy. It is **SATTVIK.**
3. **Anubuti (Spiritual experience):** While Looking at the pendant, calmness was felt and the pace of breathing became low. Pleasantness is felt.

Maharishi Adhyatma Vishwavidyalay, Goa
www.spiritual.university | e-mail: mav.research2014@gmail.com | Call: 9561574972, 8451006060

Jawahar Road, Thavakkara, Kannur-670001, Kerala, India
+91 497 2767465, 2766515, 2764514, 2764516, 2702467 8291100514
sudhacvr@gmail.com www.krishnajewelindia.com krishnajewelskannur

Krishna Beach Resort, Palliyamoola, Kannur-670008
0497 2715888, 7558887704

Payyambalam-Palliyamoola Beach Road, Kannur-670008, Kerala, India
0497 2715888, 7558887704 reservations@kbrkannur.com
om@kbrkannur.com www.kbrkannur.com krishnabeachresort

PURITY (IQ) ★ CREATIVITY (EQ) ★ SPIRITUALITY (SQ) ★ DIVINITY (DQ)

www.ingramcontent.com/pod-product-compliance
Lightning Source LLC
Chambersburg PA
CBHW022117150726
47990CB00003B/1384